WALSALL
IN OLD PHOTOGRAPHS

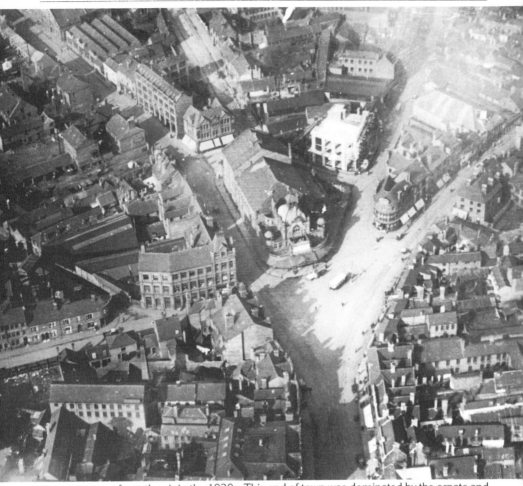

TOWN END BANK from the air in the 1930s. This end of town was dominated by the ornate and impressive Her Majesty's Theatre. The number of factories, workshops and houses squeezed into the yards behind Park Street is also notable.

WALSALL
IN OLD PHOTOGRAPHS

COLLECTED BY
MARILYN LEWIS & DOUGLAS GILBERT

ALAN SUTTON
1988

Alan Sutton Publishing Limited
Brunswick Road · Gloucester

First published 1988

British Library Cataloguing in Publication Data

Walsall in old photographs.
1. West Midlands (Metropolitan County).
Walsall, history
I. Lewis, Marilyn II. Gilbert, Douglas
942.4'92

ISBN 0-86299-436-5

Typesetting and origination by
Alan Sutton Publishing Limited
Printed in Great Britain
by WBC Print Limited.

CONTENTS

BRIDGEMAN STREET, looking towards the subway, where the road dips to allow the railway overhead. As always, St Matthew's Church dominates the skyline.

INTRODUCTION

Being tinged with the smoke and manufacturing vicinity, this town has been often looked upon with ignominy and contempt; but surely without just reason, if we may judge from its present appearance ... it surely deserves to be better known, for its lords have been some of the most eminent men in the kingdom and its situation is particularly striking, on a bold eminence, from the summit of which rises its fine old Gothic Church and lofty spire, the streets and houses gradually descending on every side.

So wrote the Reverend Stebbing Shaw in his *History and Antiquities of Staffordshire* in 1798. His words are as appropriate now as they were 200 years ago. To the newcomer, Walsall would have little to recommend it at first sight, but closer association tends to lead to an appreciation and respect for its rich and turbulent past and lively and varied present.

Walsall has been a prosperous market and manufacturing town since medieval times. The mineral wealth of the land upon which the town stands has been exploited by the inhabitants for centuries. Coal, ironstone and limestone were all mined locally and used in the production of iron and light metal goods. Until the eighteenth century, this industrial activity was carried out on a small scale but, with the coming of the canal and, later, the railway, Walsall's industries developed rapidly and at the expense of the surrounding countryside.

Walsall has always been a town of change. Its commercial and industrial prosperity has ensured that change and redevelopment should be a constant process. Agricultural land, rural villages and country houses were swallowed up by the Industrial Revolution and in the town itself houses, factories and workshops were squeezed into every available scrap of land with little regard for public health or housing standards. In the 1890s many of Walsall's medieval and Tudor buildings were swept away in favour of grand and elaborate Victorian structures. The 1930s brought a passion for 'modernism' and a reaction against the despised 'Victoriana'. The love of contemporary style and an impatience with the past sealed the fate of many more of Walsall's historic buildings in the 1960s. It is only with the 1980s that there has been an appreciation of Walsall's heritage and the need to conserve what remains of it.

It is fortunate that a number of Walsall men were conscious of the changes taking place around them and set out to record their heritage before it was too late. This was the prime motivation of five of Walsall's greatest photographers. William Bullock was a professional photographer, specialising in studio portraits in the first half of the twentieth century. He was also an active member of Walsall Photographic Society. His general shots of Walsall record much of the town's transformation in the decades before World War Two.

W.B. Shaw was an internationally renowned chemist and lectured at the Walsall Science and Art Institute. Photography was his hobby and he too was a member of the Walsall Photographic Society. The majority of Shaw's photographs which have come down to us today are copies of earlier views. In duplicating these photographs Shaw showed remarkable foresight, since in most cases it is Shaw's copies rather than the originals which have survived.

William Meikle, the third of our photographers, was born in the Black Country in c. 1860 of Scottish ancestry – he was proud of both facts. He was, perhaps, the first

THE VIEW TOWARDS ST MATTHEW'S CHURCH from the Dolphin Inn, in George Street. The inn sign can be seen on the gable end.

of our five photographers to appreciate fully the historical significance of his work. He was certainly meticulous in recording dates and other details, which suggests that he was aware that his photographs would have a longer life than he, himself. Meikle bequeathed to Walsall Council a huge collection of photographic negatives, lantern slides, sketches, anecdotes and reminiscences on many aspects of the history of the town and other West Midlands towns and villages. A credit draper by occupation, he had occasion to make many business trips around the Midlands, on which he picked up much of his collection of historical artefacts and *objets d'art*. Meikle was a sociable man and frequented many of Walsall's public houses. He deplored the tendency of turn-of-the-century breweries to impose a common style on their houses – he called them 'chromium plated gin palaces' – and undertook to record the original character of Walsall's ancient inns. He was also the first photographer to turn away from the main streets of the town and concentrate on the back streets and slums of Victorian Walsall.

Douglas Gilbert, co-author of this book and the fourth of our photographers, knew his three predecessors and their work. When he entered the family business – Gilbert and Son, estate agents and auctioneers – one of his tasks was to collect rent from the properties in the care of the firm, including many of the ancient buildings in the centre of the town. Born in 1910, as a young man in the 1930s and an enthusiastic member of the Photographic Society, he was in a position to know that most of the houses and shops at the heart of the town which he visited every week were due for demolition and he undertook to record them for posterity. Douglas Gilbert's passion for architecture is evident in his photographs – recording the doomed buildings of Walsall was his intention, but many of his photographs capture local people in a most spontaneous and engaging fashion.

Douglas Gilbert qualified for the Estate profession in 1933, when he joined his father's practice. One of his early responsibilities was to collect rents from the slum properties on the Church Hill. The squalor of the ancient buildings was indescribable. Mr Gilbert recently told his co-author that the stench of a Moroccan souk was as nothing compared to that of the houses of Upper Rushall Street.

Mr Gilbert, who has held many chairmanships, professional and otherwise, retired from business in 1975. A past President of Walsall Photographic Society and President of the Walsall Association of the National Trust, he is still an enthusiastic protector of his town's heritage.

Our final photographer is Jack Haddock, a resident of North Walsall with a passion for all forms of transport. A fanatical train-spotter from childhood and, later, an employee of Walsall Corporation Transport Department, he has been photographing trains, trams, trolleys, canal boats and motor vehicles in the town for 30 years. More recently, he has recorded the demolition of historic sites, such as Walsall station and the George Hotel and compiled a bank of oral history tapes, all now deposited with Walsall Local History Centre.

At first sight, Walsall may seem a nondescript town, blessed with few buildings of architectural merit and, indeed, it must be conceded that the town has sacrificed most of its finest buildings. But it is, in fact, the people of Walsall which make it special. Their tolerant good humour and dry, deadpan wit, continue to win them the respect and affection of visitors and newcomers.

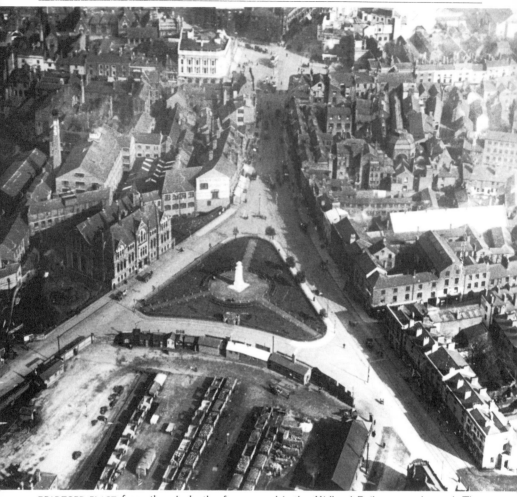

BRADFORD PLACE from the air. In the foreground is the Midland Railway goods yard. The cenotaph can be seen in the centre of the picture.

Growing Up

BABY SHOW at the Town Hall in 1921. The winner, out of 350 babies, was Frederick Coates. His mother received a cup, presented by Alderman C.C. Walker.

BLOXWICH JMI SCHOOL, class I, c. 1919.

WHITEHALL JUNIOR SCHOOL STANDARD III CLASS in the early twentieth century. A typical classroom interior of the period. On the blackboard at the back of the class are the names of two children who came top in an arithmetic test — Edna Hattersley and Donald Moffat.

NORTH WALSALL INFANTS SCHOOL, Class II, c. 1930. There were 58 pupils in this class.

NORTH WALSALL JUNIOR SCHOOL Standard IV girls' class, 1922. North Walsall was opened after the 1902 Education Act, to serve the growing population of North Walsall and Ryecroft.

BOYS' WOODWORK CLASS. In c. 1930 a series of photographs was taken of the pupils at work at Bloxwich JMI School.

GIRLS' HANDICRAFTS CLASS.

GIRLS' HANDICRAFTS CLASS. Most of the girls are working with raffia and cane.

COOKERY CLASS.

PE. CLASS.

CHURCH HILL at the turn of the century. The children are pupils of the Blue Coat School, which was located in a building adjacent to St Matthew's Church.

QUEEN MARY'S GRAMMAR SCHOOL was founded in 1554. The school moved into these premises in 1850. A Girls' High School was opened on an adjacent site in 1893. When the Grammar moved to a new site in Gorway in 1965, the High School took over these buildings.

WISEMORE, looking east from Stafford Street, 1937. There were no parks or open spaces in the area for children to play in.

NEW STREET in 1936. The poverty of the residents of this area is indicated by the clothes of the two girls standing in the road.

GORTON'S YARD on Church Hill, 1936. This must have been an unhealthy and difficult place to bring up children.

UPPER RUSHALL STREET, 1936. With no back gardens to speak of, these children had to play in the street – 'tip cat', marbles and similar inexpensive games were popular.

A CHRISTMAS PARTY, such as this one in 1939, was a special treat for the children of Walsall's poorer population.

TOWN END BANK, 1937, after demolition of Her Majesty's Theatre. The girls are running towards an ice cream seller. Dicico, Pelari and Pisuto were all Italian emigrants who settled in Walsall prior to World War One and set up ice cream businesses.

SECTION TWO

At Home

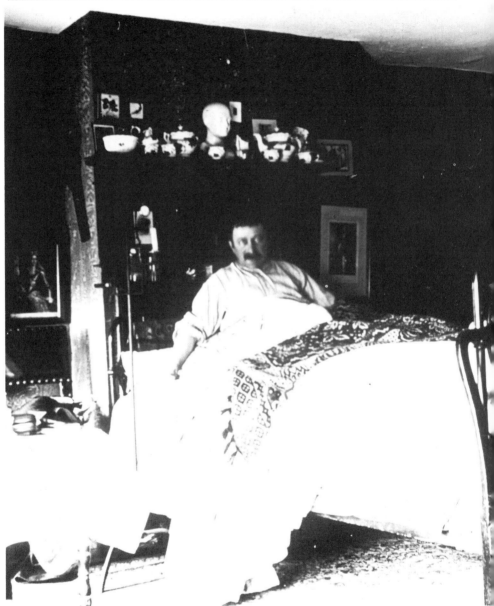

BILLY MEIKLE in his bedroom at No. 26 Lichfield Street. Meikle was born c. 1860 in Tipton, but lived for most of his life in Walsall.

ANOTHER VIEW OF THE PHOTOGRAPHER'S BEDROOM, with his clothes scattered around a chair.

THE PARLOUR contained ample evidence of Meikle's mania for collecting. A large and varied collection of china is on display, picked up by Meikle on his business travels as a credit draper.

MEIKLE'S HOUSE was full of books, photographs and objects which bore testimony to his antiquarian interests.

MANY OF MEIKLE'S FINEST PIECES were bargains obtained from customers unaware of their true worth. The dresser was acquired from a family using it as a rabbit hutch – for the price of the rabbit!

THE KITCHEN AT MEIKLE'S HOUSE, showing an attractive iron range and an impressive collection of pewter or brass ornaments. The gas light fitting is clearly visible here.

AN ATTRACTIVE CORNER CABINET displaying more of Meikle's china. The highly decorated picture rail is most unusual.

THIS LITTLE FARMHOUSE IN RUSHALL was photographed by Meikle in 1900.

COTTAGES AT SANDBANK, Bloxwich, 1938.

SMALL COTTAGES at Sandbank, Bloxwich, 1937.

A THATCHED COTTAGE in Bell Lane, Bloxwich, 1938, with a poster advertising the Odeon Cinema in Bloxwich. Although only a minute's walk from the centre of Bloxwich, this scene has a distinctly rural atmosphere.

DINNER PARTY at Bescot Hall, c. 1910. The owner, Samuel Mills Slater, is seated with his back to the camera. Mr Slater was Mayor of Walsall during World War One. His wife died from injuries received in the Zeppelin raid on the town on 31 January 1916.

LOWER RUSHALL STREET, 1936. Once handsome and fashionable residences of the well-to-do. By the thirties these houses were derelict and insanitary.

HOUSES IN A COURT behind Lower Rushall Street, 1937, with shared toilets and water supply. Most industrial towns had many courts of this kind.

THE REAR OF THE HOUSES IN LOWER RUSHALL STREET, 1937, after demolition of the courts had begun. The houses were ancient, dilapidated and insanitary.

THE DEMOLITION OF HOUSES on the south-east side of Lower Rushall Street in 1937. The house in the courtyard, on the right of our photograph, was still occupied while the demolition took place around it. The timber-frame construction of the house next door is clearly visible.

REAR OF HOUSES IN PARK STREET backing on to the railway line, September 1914. The photographer has attracted the attention of some children who are watching him from a ground-floor window.

DUDLEY STREET, 1936, looking towards the junction with Bath Street.

DEMOLITION OF HOUSES in Cowley's Yard behind Birmingham Street, 1936. The cramped and insanitary housing on Church Hill was demolished in phases between the 1890s and 1950s.

SECTION THREE
At Work

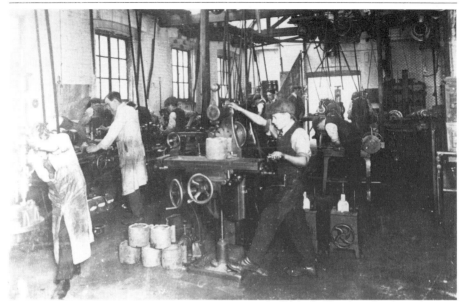

INTERIOR OF AN UNIDENTIFIED METAL GOODS FACTORY in Walsall. Metal trades have been a feature of the town's commercial life since the Middle Ages.

THE WORKSHOP OF J.C. CULWICK, ornamental and 'medieval' metalworker in the late nineteenth century. Walsall had many such self-employed craftsmen, as well as the foundries and factories for which it was best known.

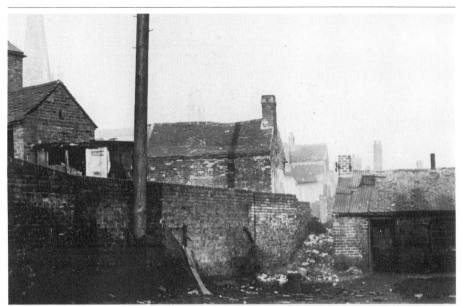

BEHIND NO. 28 BIRMINGHAM STREET stood Walsall's smallest factory – as defined by the Factories Act. Mr A. Dutton ran his pattern-making business from this little building.

INTERIOR OF A NAIL-MAKING FACTORY behind Walsall Technical College prior to its demolition in the 1950s. A large industrial bellows can be seen.

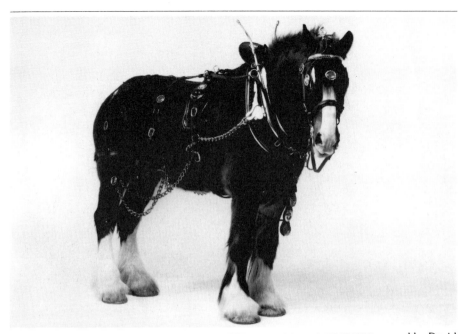

SHIRE GELDING 'VISCOUNT', owned by David Lewis of Walsall Horse & Cart Gear (1986) Ltd, wearing a full set of show harness. Walsall has been a centre of horse harness manufacture for centuries. The town was known for this industry long before its famous saddlery trade became so important (*Bryan Holden Collection*).

THE BRITISH & COLONIAL HORSE SHOE AND MACHINE COMPANY STAND at a trade fair. The company, which was based at the Globe Ironworks in Charles Street, was one of many Walsall businesses specialising in saddlers' ironmongery.

BLOXWICH LOCK & STAMPING CO. LTD. was established in 1915. Both photographs date from the thirties and several workers occur in both pictures.

GEORGE MADELEY, of G.H.T Madeley & Co., leather glove manufacturers in Station Street, c. 1935. On the desk is the original glove produced by the company in 1920.

THE FIRM OF WHITEHOUSE COX, leather goods manufacturers based in Marsh Street, was owned c. 1935 by Mrs E. Cox, seen here in the Works Director's Office.

GLOVE-MAKING at Whitehouse Cox Ltd., c. 1935.

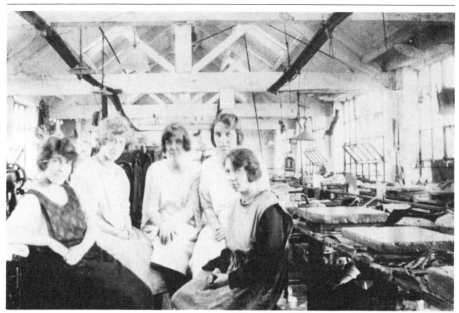

FACTORY GIRLS inside the premises of John More, fancy leather goods manufacturer in Wolverhampton Street, before 1928.

INSIDE EDGAR STAMMER'S CLOTHING FACTORY in New Street, c. 1920.

WALSALL ABOUNDED IN MINERAL RESOURCES — limestone, ironstone and coal were all mined locally. Most of the mines were small-scale and independently owned. Meikle photographed this mine in Rushall in the early twentieth century.

A FAINT BUT RARE PHOTOGRAPH OF BENTLEY HALL. Once the elegant home of the Lane family, coal mines encroached on its land and eventually came right up to the front door. A number of former homes of Walsall's gentry were lost in the Industrial Revolution's search for mineral wealth — Reynold's Hall, in what is now the Arboretum, for example.

WALSALL'S FIRST POWER STATION, the Birchills electricity generating station, was built between 1914 and 1916.

AT THE HEART OF THE COUNTRY'S CANAL NETWORK, Walsall once had many boat builders. The last, Peter Keay & Son at Pratt's Bridge, was making wooden boats in the traditional way until the early 1980s.

NO. 19 GOODALL STREET, 1938. The premises of a cooper and packing case maker.

PINFOLD, Bloxwich, 1937. The building on the left was Alf Sergeant's barber's shop. He charged 1d. per haircut. One day he offered free shaves and tried to shave as many men as possible – his total was 40.

RYECROFT FARM was bought by Walsall Council in 1919 and the land used for one of the town's first council estates.

SECTION FOUR

Having Fun

BLOXWICH WAKES 18 August 1908. A Wake has been held at Bloxwich for at least 200 years. This couple and their pony and carriage appeared as a sideshow at Pat Collins' fair.

THE GRAND THEATRE had opened in 1890 on a prominent site at the corner of Park Street and Station Street. It was destroyed in a dramatic fire in 1939.

THE SITE HAD BEEN OCCUPIED BY THE GAIETY THEATRE prior to 1890. Although the structure was not totally rebuilt, the elaborate façade of the Grand bore little resemblance to the plainer Gaiety.

HER MAJESTY'S THEATRE was opened in 1900. It was converted into a cinema in 1933 and demolished in 1937. The shops on the right of the photograph include J. Frisby Ltd., boot dealer, T. Sheen, baker and confectioner and the imposing building at the end of the row was a post office, formerly Park Hall House.

AFTER HER MAJESTY'S WAS DEMOLISHED, a modern cinema, The Savoy, was built on the site the following year.

UPPER BRIDGE STREET in 1924. The billboard is advertising a film starring silent movie star Harold Lloyd.

BRIDGE STREET, WALSALL.

THE PICTURE HOUSE in Bridge Street. Work began on this building before World War One, but it did not open until 1920. Known as the Gaumont from 1948 and the Odeon from 1965, this cinema was destroyed by fire in 1923 and 1971.

WALSALL FC was formed in 1888, upon the amalgamation of two clubs – Town and Swifts. A training session at Fellows Park, 1927.

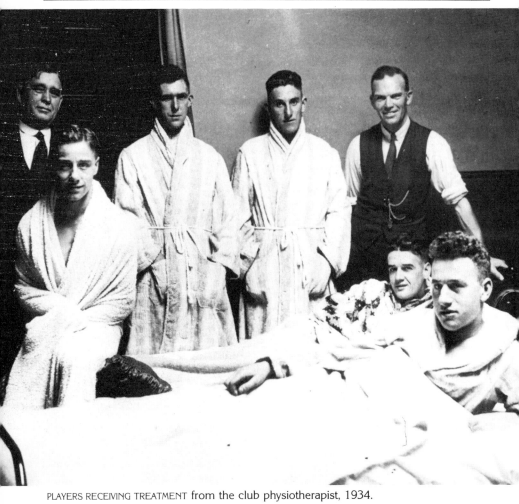

PLAYERS RECEIVING TREATMENT from the club physiotherapist, 1934.

THE TEAM RUN OUT FOR A MATCH in the 1930s. Police officers line the path as the players come out through the densely packed crowd. Fellows Park was a claustrophobic ground for visiting teams, with supporters crowding in close to the pitch on three sides and the wall of Orgill's laundry on the other side.

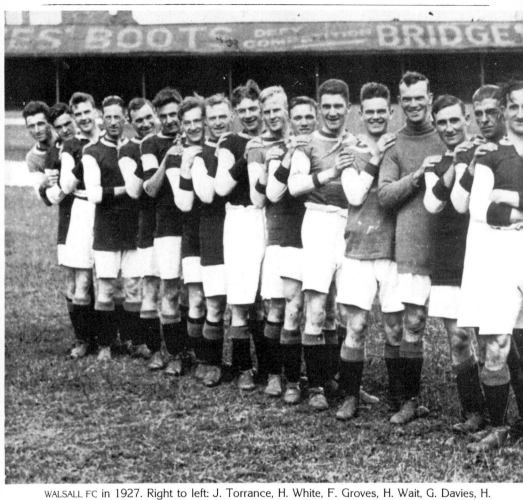

WALSALL FC in 1927. Right to left: J. Torrance, H. White, F. Groves, H. Wait, G. Davies, H. Beck, B. Scholes, F. Binks, J. Walker, T. Holt, G. Pumford, J. Bancroft, G. Smith, E. Parry, H. Alcock, W. Bradford, A. Rawlings.

WALSALL FC on tour in Holland. The team which beat Arsenal in 1933 outside their hotel with one of the club's directors, Mr Roper. The defeat of Arsenal in the FA Cup in 1933 was Walsall's greatest footballing triumph for half a century. It is only in recent years that the club's achievements have surpassed that great day.

WALSALL FC RESERVES, 1943–4 season.

THE ARBORETUM, opened in 1870, provided a welcome open space and recreation area in the centre of Walsall. The Arboretum was originally run by a private company and an admission charge was levied.

'HEALTH AND BEAUTY' EVENTS were a feature of the 1930s. This demonstration took place at Fellows Park.

THE REAR OF THE VINE INN, Lower Hall Lane, in the early twentieth century. One of the group is holding a snooker or billiard cue. The dog, perhaps used for ratting, has a bandaged leg. The writing on the tray reads 'Sgts. Mess 4th Man[chester] Regiment.'

THE PUBLIC BAR OF THE BOROUGH ARMS, Upper Rushall Street.

THE QUEEN'S HOTEL in Station Street. Note the attractive decoration above the windows on the upper floors.

THE CROWN INN, Long Acre Street, after 1920.

THE CONSTRUCTION OF WALSALL WORKING MEN'S CLUB, at the corner of Cobden Street and Milton Street, Palfrey, c. 1911–12.

MEIKLE AND SOME OF HIS FRIENDS in his local, the British Oak, in Lichfield Street. Note the spitoon on the floor.

ALL THE REGULARS seem to have come outside for this photograph of the Spring Cottage Inn in Shelfield, c. 1928.

MANY READERS will remember street parties to celebrate the end of World War Two, such as this one in Queen Street.

In The Street

THE VIEW DOWN HIGH STREET in 1937. Walsall's main street since the Middle Ages, its buildings have been demolished and reconstructed in the contemporary style by almost every generation.

THROUGH THE LYCH GATE OF ST MATTHEW'S CHURCH, 1936. The shops, houses and inns, such as the Leathern Bottle, came much closer to the church than the buildings on the Hill today. The Hill was gradually cleared of its slums between the 1890s and early 1950s.

HIGH STREET, looking down Digbeth towards the Bridge. Two of Walsall's oldest inns, the Talbot and the Old Still, are visible.

A RARE PHOTOGRAPH of the attractive row of houses which ran down Church Hill, towards the top of High Street. The houses were demolished in the early years of this century.

THE JUNCTION OF NEW STREET AND DUDLEY STREET in 1936. Demolition of the centuries-old buildings was well under way. To the right can be seen the Duke of York Inn, which was to be demolished the following year.

THE SAME JUNCTION looking from Dudley Street towards Church Street about 30 years earlier.

LOOKING DOWN DUDLEY STREET, past the White Swan on the left, c. 1930. This narrow street was the main route out of the town westwards to Dudley.

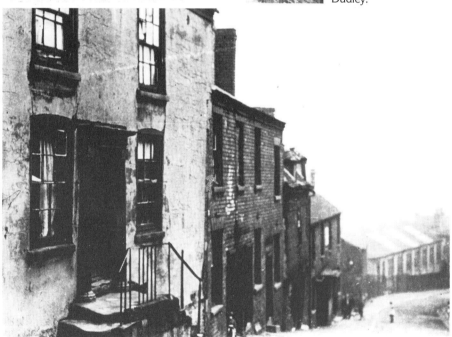

HILL STREET, 1936; one of Walsall's original medieval streets, it had fallen into disrepair by the time this photograph was taken.

THE BRIDGE, C. 1895–1900. Walsall's first Bridge was a little wooden structure over the Walsall Brook. By the 1870s it had been covered over to form an impressive public square.

AN EARLY TWENTIETH-CENTURY VIEW of the Bridge, showing the clock presented by Mr F. B. Oerton, Mayor in 1854–5.

DIGBETH, looking towards High Street in 1939, an attractive street of eighteenth- and nineteenth-century façades now, sadly, lost.

WALSALL BROOK behind Hatherton Street, c. 1910. The brook flows right under the town centre.

BENEATH THE BRIDGE in the early twentieth century.

BRADFORD STREET was opened in 1831. Note the horse trough to the left. All the buildings behind have now been demolished.

BRADFORD ST., (1) WALSALL. NO. 786.

A CLOSER LOOK AT BRADFORD STREET, showing the Arcade, built in 1892.

AN AERIAL VIEW OF WOLVERHAMPTON STREET in the early thirties. Goods traffic can be seen on the canal on the right and, again, the typical mixture of housing cheek by jowl with industrial premises is evident.

ST PAUL'S STREET looking towards Wisemore in 1936. McManus' grocer's shop is visible on the right.

WISEMORE, 1936. Site of one of Walsall's common fields in the Middle Ages, Wisemore was densely built up by the early nineteenth century.

HOUSES IN BIRMINGHAM STREET, 1936. The stone high on the wall was moved from another building in the street and commemorates the home of the Stone family who were prominent in the seventeenth century.

THE JUNCTION OF BIRMINGHAM ROAD AND ABLEWELL STREET, showing the Walsall House Inn, 1936.

UPPER RUSHALL STREET, 1936, showing the Borough Arms on the left and an attractive row of eighteenth-century buildings.

LOWER RUSHALL STREET in the 1930s was a mixture of houses, shops and factories. Several buildings had been converted into poor quality lodging houses.

THE DE-LICENSED SHAKESPEARE INN, at the corner of Church Hill and Peal Street. St Matthew's Church steps can be seen in the foreground.

DEMOLITION OF THE OLD QUEEN'S HEAD on Church Hill to make way for the St Matthew's Church Institute, opened c. 1903.

THE OLD DOG INN, Pool Street had been de-licensed by the time this photograph was taken in 1937.

LOWER BRIDGE STREET, 1933, showing Grey's department store at the entrance to the Old Square and the Bridge Street Congregational Church, which was demolished in 1966.

A MID TWENTIETH-CENTURY PHOTOGRAPH looking along Park Street before pedestrianisation. St Matthew's Church stands alone on the skyline. In a similar view today the church would be dwarfed by blocks of flats.

UPPER BRIDGE STREET before 1927, during demolition of the nineteenth-century buildings prior to construction of the new Co-operative Society premises.

ST PAUL'S STREET prior to the creation of the new bus station. In the centre of the photograph can be seen the bell tower of the Blue Coat School.

WOLVERHAMPTON STREET, showing the back of Her Majesty's Theatre, 1937.

ADAMS ROW, 1936 – early nineteenth-century shops and houses.

STAFFORD STREET, 1936. Although a few minutes' walk from the town centre, Stafford Street was a thriving commercial centre in its own right.

THE ARBORETUM LAKES are flooded limestone workings – an outcrop of limestone is visible. The handsome villa residences of Victoria Terrace, built for Walsall's new élite in the 1850s can be seen above.

BLOXWICH HIGH STREET in the early twentieth century. Two miles north of Walsall, the town of Bloxwich has been closely linked with its larger neighbour by commercial, social and administrative ties for many centuries.

CALDMORE ROAD in the early twentieth century. Caldmore was an outlying settlement of Walsall from at least the fourteenth century. Although the town grew out to absorb it, the area still retains its own character.

SECTION SIX

Shops

WALSALL MARKET in the 1950s. There has been a market on this site since the thirteenth century. Livestock, especially pigs, formed an important part of market trade for many centuries.

PARK STREET in the early twentieth century. The old fish shop is boarded up and the site offered for sale – the premises were to be rebuilt. Note the wooden window shutters.

PARK STREET in the early twentieth century showing (left to right) True-Form Boot Co., Burton, the tailors and the Station Hotel.

BADHAM'S BAKERS SHOP in Church Street, Bloxwich, in the early years of the twentieth century. This photograph is of interest as an illustration of an Edwardian shop frontage and of the dress of the staff and customers.

A NEWSAGENT AND CONFECTIONERY SHOP in Green Lane at the turn of the century. Shops such as this stocked a huge variety of goods on their small, cluttered premises.

IN CONTRAST are the smart staff and well-designed displays of this Co-op branch.

INSIDE THE ARCADE, looking towards Bradford Street, showing Westwood's baby shop and Davies' 'athletic outfitters'.

STANTON'S GREENGROCERY BUSINESS, in Upper Rushall Street, survives today as Welling's, although few other shops or houses remain in the street.

DUDLEY STREET, c. 1936, showing the premises of B. Scoltock, chimney sweep – note the traditional sweep's sign over the door – and the medieval timber-framed Duke of York next door.

THE THORNHILL FAMILY lived at 19 New Street on Church Hill. Nearby Joseph Thornhill established a pawnbrokers business in the late nineteenth century. The shop was well located. Most residents of the Church Hill area were poor and made much use of pawnbrokers.

JOSEPH THORNHILL died c. 1880, but his wife Ann carried on the business with her children. Ann survived her husband by almost 30 years.

THE THORNHILLS' PAWNBROKERS SHOP at the corner of Gortons Yard and New Street. One of Mrs Thornhill's sons is seen in the doorway.

THIS BOOT REPAIR SHOP at 42 New Street was owned by the Thornhill family.

TAYLOR'S MUSIC SHOP in Lower Bridge Street is a familiar sight to Walsall residents. Although the shop closed in the mid-1980s, few local people have failed to notice the lovely terracotta carvings on the façade of the building. Our photograph shows the shop interior in the early twentieth century.

THE WORKSHOP AT TAYLOR'S, where they repaired musical instruments. The firm was established in the mid-nineteenth century.

CO-OP BRANCH 7 in Walsall Wood High Street was opened in 1903. Our photograph dates from c. 1910.

HORSE-DRAWN DELIVERY VANS were used by Walsall & District Co-op until after World War Two.

THIS MOTOR VAN is shown outside the Upper Bridge Street store in c. 1935.

A HORSE-DRAWN FLOAT produced by Walsall & District Co-operative Society to promote its boot repair service.

THE SERVICE WAS STARTED IN 1906 and operated from this factory in Hollyhedge Lane.

Government, Order and Religion

THIS PHOTOGRAPH TAKEN in 1938, shows the moat of Walsall's medieval manor house, looking towards Wilbraham Street. The site has now been obliterated by extensions to the Manor Hospital.

TEDDESLEY HOUSE, C. 1890, where the Town Hall now stands. Walsall Fire Brigade was formed in 1879, although the town maintained a modest engine from the late eighteenth century.

THE TOWN HALL was built in Lichfield Street between 1902–1905. The tower, seen here during its construction, has contained a carillon since 1953.

"Carnegie" Library and Town Hall, Walsall.

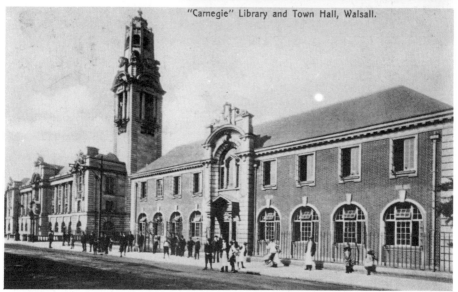

THE LIBRARY was opened in 1906, funded by Andrew Carnegie, next door to the Town Hall.

THE *OBSERVER* OFFICE stood next to the George Hotel on the Bridge. The *Walsall Observer* was established in 1868 by John and William Griffin, who ran a printing business from the same premises.

THE GEORGE HOTEL stood on the Bridge at the corner of Digbeth. It was demolished and rebuilt between 1933 and 1935 and demolished again in 1979.

LOBBY OF THE GEORGE HOTEL, C. 1900. A North Western Railway timetable can be seen on the wall.

BILLY MEIKLE took this photograph of the barmaid of the George Hotel bar, C. 1900.

ST MATTHEW'S CHURCH, C. 1905, seen from the top of the Guildhall. The church dates from
c. 1200, but was largely rebuilt between 1819–1821.

THE BELLS OF ST MATTHEW'S CHURCH in the early twentieth century. The present bells were recast in 1928–9. The church also had a chiming clock from the mid-fifteenth century.

ST GEORGE'S CHURCH, at the junction of Persehouse Street and Walhouse Road, was built in 1873–5, but demolished in 1964.

THE UNITARIAN CHURCH in Stafford Street was opened in 1827, replacing an earlier meeting house in Bank Court, just off High Street.

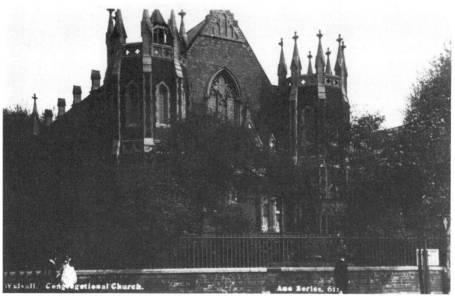

THE CONGREGATIONAL CHURCH in Wednesbury Road was opened in 1858. Partly rebuilt after bomb damage during the 1916 Zeppelin raid, the church was demolished in 1973.

THE INTERIOR OF THE BAPTIST CHAPEL in Stafford Street in the late nineteenth century. The Ebenezer chapel was built in 1846 and not replaced until 1972, when a new church was opened in Green Lane.

BLAKENALL CHURCH OF ENGLAND SUNDAY SCHOOL, 1898, showing the infants and elder children-cum-teachers.

BLOXWICH POLICE c. 1928. At that time the entire Walsall Force consisted of one Chief Constable, one Chief Inspector, one Inspector, four Patrol Inspectors, one Detective Sergeant, 10 Sergeants, four Detective Constables and 89 Constables.

A MEETING OF WALSALL SCHOOL BOARD in their Bradford Street premises in 1896. Left to right: Revd George Barrans, Walter Checketts, Revd W.R. Carlyon, Revd P. Dean, Miss M. Disturnal, W. Walford, R.H. Hulme, Revd J.C. Hamilton, Revd W.S. Swayne (later Bishop of Lincoln), Enoch Evans, A. Jeffries, J. Thorpe and Miss E. Brace.

OFFICERS AND NCO'S of the first Volunteer Battalion of the South Staffordshire Regiment Special Service Corps during World War One.

5th BATTALION OF THE SOUTH STAFFORDSHIRE REGIMENT with their colours, 1910.

A BRITISH LEGION SERVICE in the Aboretum grandstand in September 1933.

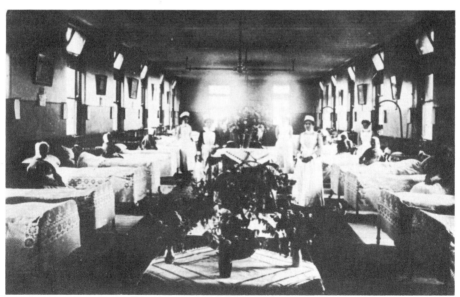

THE WOMEN'S WARD in the Workhouse, 1910. The ward was gas lit – note the pipes. All the inmates are wearing standard issue dresses and caps.

Transport

A SIGHT TO STIR THE BLOOD OF ANY STEAM ENTHUSIAST. Three locomotives moving away from Walsall Station, passing Long Street *en route* to Bescot.

PLATFORM ONE, WALSALL STATION, c. 1958. Walsall's first station had opened at Bescot Bridge in 1837. A town centre station did not follow until 1847.

PLATFORM ONE, WALSALL STATION, 1957. The Jinty is taking on water. In the background can be seen the distinctive round booking hall, which was demolished in 1979.

VIEW FROM THE TAMEWAY TOWER at Town End, looking across Walsall Station.

A BOOKING HALL was opened in Park Street in 1884. It was burnt down in 1916. The new circular hall opened on 4 November 1923. Mr J.F. Bradford, District Superintendent of the London & North Western Railway Company is shown opening the doors.

WORKS TO WIDEN THE BRIDGE over the railway at St Paul's Street, 1937.

THE COAL PLANT at the Bescot sidings, 1957.

Above right,
THE STEAM LOCOMOTIVE *SISTER DORA*, probably at Monument Lane, Birmingham. Named after Walsall's great heroine, she was in service between Derby–Burton–Lichfield–Sutton Coldfield–Birmingham–Walsall.

Below right,
STEPHENSON LOCOMOTIVE SOCIETY SPECIAL seen at Walsall, c. 1961. Some of the steam enthusiasts can be seen on the platform admiring the locomotive.

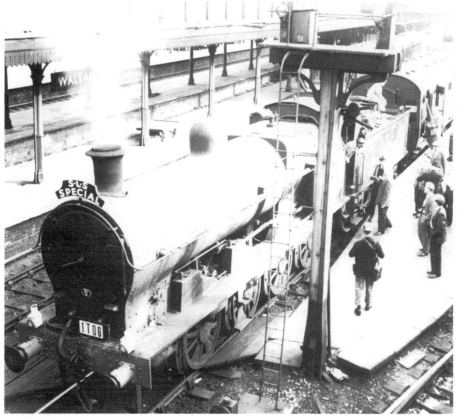

NORTH WALSALL JUNCTION SIGNAL BOX, C. 1959.

RUSHALL CROSSING SIGNAL BOX, C. 1980.

LAUNCHING THE BOAT *MEROPE* in snow at Keay's dock, December 1978.

'MAC' PULLING THE LAST HORSE-DRAWN CANAL BOAT in Walsall, *Eddie*, at the Walsall Locks in 1965.

TUG *JUDITH ANN* passing the spelter works near Bloxwich Lane, c. 1960–2. Steering the boat is a great Black Country character 'Caggy' Stevens.

THE CANAL came to Walsall in 1799. It transported raw materials, such as limestone and manufactured goods from Walsall and brought in commodities such as sugar. Working boats were still a common sight on the local canals well into this century.

TRAM NO. 40 outside the electricity generating station at Darlaston Road in the early twentieth century.

ELECTRIC TRAMS were introduced to Walsall in 1892. Walsall was one of the first towns in Britain to introduce an electrified tramway system. Car 39 is seen here approaching the Bridge.

A GANG OF WORKMEN taking up the tramlines in Wednesbury Road after trams were withdrawn in 1933.

ONE OF WALSALL'S DISTINCTIVE BLUE TROLLEYBUSES passing the Wesleyan Chapel in Leamore in c. 1960. Trolleybuses were first introduced in Walsall in 1931. They were gradually withdrawn in favour of motor buses between 1965 and 1970.

TOWN END BANK, c. 1960. Trolleybuses caused considerable traffic congestion at this notorious bottleneck.

A PONY AND TRAP in the yard behind Stanton's greengrocers, of Upper Rushall Street in the early twentieth century.

THIS DELIVERY CART belonged to Mr A. Simms, who bottled and sold ale, porter (a stronger brew) and pop. He operated from the old racecourse grandstand.

THIS MOTOR CAR bearing an early Walsall number plate, belonged to Mr Francis Hodgkinson of West Bromwich Street. His pride in his new car is evident in this photograph.

THE ST PAUL'S STREET BUS STATION opened in 1935. St Paul's Terrace, long since demolished, is visible on the far right.

THE TAME VALLEY, C. 1960, looking towards Walsall Power Station in the distance. The M6 motorway has now transformed this landscape. This stretch opened in 1968.

People

SISTER DORA, born Dorothy Wyndlow Pattison in 1832, came to Walsall for the first time in early 1865 to work in the town's new Cottage Hospital. From November 1865 she was in charge and earned the respect and love of the town's population. A pioneer of casualty nursing techniques, her death from cancer in 1878 plunged the whole town into mourning. Walsall's greatest citizen has, perhaps, never received the national recognition her achievements deserved.

THE TOWN SUBSCRIBED TO THIS MARBLE STATUE OF SISTER DORA which was unveiled on the Bridge in 1886. Pollution badly damaged the stone over the years and it was substituted by a bronze replica in 1957. This photograph was taken the day after the unveiling ceremony – the four carved scenes from Sister Dora's life in Walsall had yet to be added to the pedestal.

THE IDENTITY OF THIS VICTORIAN GROUP IS NOT KNOWN. They are clearly wearing their best clothes for the occasion.

AMY JOHNSON in her plane Kirby Kite. Miss Johnson had a dramatic crash when she visited Walsall Aerodrome, but emerged unscathed.

THE TOMB OF SIR ROGER HILLARY OF BESCOT, who died in 1356. The Hillary family lived at the original Bescot Hall.

THOMAS FLETCHER, founder of the George Hotel, Walsall's premier coaching inn, established in 1781.

THE WEDDING OF LILIAN AND ROLAND HOLMES in the early twentieth century. The couple kept the Durham Ox public house for a number of years, and later, the Brown Lion in Pleck. This clear view of the wedding group's clothes is particularly interesting.

AN UNIDENTIFIED WALSALL FAMILY of the Victorian period. Three generations of this clearly prosperous family can be seen in the photograph.

SECTION TEN

Events

THE FOUNDATION STONE of the new Town Hall was laid by Prince Christian of Schleswig-Holstein in 1902. Afterwards he attended a banquet in the Public Baths building.

STAFF AND VOLUNTEERS of the Walsall & District section of the Staffordshire branch of the British Red Cross Society on the Bridge during World War One.

THE LARGE OPEN SPACE OF THE BRIDGE was a natural choice for ceremonial occasions. Here the mayor is reading the proclamation of the accession of King George V in 1910.

THE BAND OF THE SOUTH STAFFORDSHIRE REGIMENT at Ypres during World War One. Over 12,000 Walsall men served in the war and more than 2,000 died.

WALSALL TANK WEEK was held in March 1918 as a sales drive for War Savings Certificates and War Bonds.

WALSALL TANK WEEK · THE MAYOR'S CONTRIBUTION.

THE MAYOR, S. M. SLATER, makes his contribution at Walsall's Tank Bank during World War One.

141

THE STATION on 11 June 1927 under water. Similar, albeit less spectacular, floods occurred until very recently.

UPPER BRIDGE STREET, Sunday 14 June 1931. The flood was caused by record rainfall – two inches in 45 minutes.

THIS FLOOD IN PARK STREET attracted the inevitable group of children. Note the traditional Boots the Chemist shop.

THE BRIDGEMAN STREET SUBWAY was prone to flooding. The children seem fascinated by this record flood of 1931.

BLOXWICH HOME GUARD during World War Two. First row, left to right: –?–, –?–, Lieut. Parkes, Major Wilkes, Lieut. Talbot, 2nd Lieut. Ball.

ACKNOWLEDGEMENTS

The authors would like to thank all those whose photographs have been used in the compilation of this book: In particular Mr Jack Haddock and Mr Malcolm Wilson, who generously allowed us to copy photographs from their fine collections.

Mr Ernie Genders • Mrs Forsyth • Mr H. Godwin • Mr G. Merrett • Mr J. Hooper
Mr N. Maddeley • Mr Squires • Mrs Ann French • Mrs M. Jones • Mrs Middleton
Mr Burwell • Mrs M. Hayward • Mrs Coates • Mr & Mrs Leese • Mr Butt
Mrs M. Brookes • Mr Jason Lloyd • Mrs M. Robottom • Mr H. W. Davies
Mrs N. Alsop • Mr E. Clarke • Mr Massey • Mr E. Holmes • Mr Bryan Holden
Mr G. Thompson • Mrs Hickman • Mr J. S. Webb • Mr G. Taylor
Mr J. C. Slater • Mr M. McDevitt.

All photographs are in the holdings of the Walsall Local History Centre, Essex Street, North Walsall. We are most grateful to Richard Bond, Archivist & Local Studies Officer and his staff for their assistance, most notably Stuart Williams for his excellent photography.